The wheels on the bus

The wheels on the bus go round and round,
Round and round, round and round.
The wheels on the bus go round and round,
Over the city streets.

The mums on the bus go chatter and chatter,
Chatter and chatter, chatter and chatter.
The mums on the bus go chatter and chatter,
Over the city streets.

The dads on the bus go nod and nod,
Nod and nod, nod and nod.
The dads on the bus go nod and nod,
Over the city streets.

The kids on the bus go up and down,
Up and down, up and down.
The kids on the bus go up and down,
Over the city streets.

Driving the bus

Sing the song.
Mime the actions.

Make a space in the classroom.
Pretend you are all on a bus.

Take it in turns to be the driver.

The driver needs to be able to see out of his back window. Why?

The driver doesn't want to turn round all the time so what does he do to solve his problem?
He uses a mirror.

Where does the driver need to position the mirror so that he or she can see behind?
Overhead? Round a corner?

Take it in turns to hold the mirror in place for the driver.

Can the driver see?
Off we go!

Fun with mirrors

Look at a car.

* How many mirrors are there?
* Where are they all?
* What can the driver see through them?
* Why are they all there?

Collect

things which act as mirrors

metal spoons   saucepan   wide knives

What else can we see ourselves in?

Activity 3

Problem solving 1

Get on board your bus again.
Sing the song.

Problem
Three more passengers
need to get on the bus.
How can you fit them
on?

Think about the
problem.
Test your ideas.

Think about the good points
of the ideas.

Think about the bad points
of the ideas.

Have you thought
of a round bus?

Try it out in the
classroom.

Where would the
driver go?

Get around in a bus!

Problem solving 2

Get on your bus.
Sing the song.

Problem

People want to carry large bags on to the bus.

What bags do people want to carry on to the bus? Think up some ideas.

Take it in turns to get on to your bus carrying something.

Carry some heavy bags of shopping onto your bus.

Test whether it is hard or easy to get on board.

✳ What are the problems?
✳ How could they be solved?

You could be trying to board a bus with a push-chair.

Think about where you could put the push-chair.

Test your solutions.

✳ What are the problems?
✳ How could they be solved?

Activity 5

Planning to make a bus

Why do buses look the way they do?

What do you need to know before you start making a bus?
Ask yourself some questions about buses.

* Why have they got big wheels?
* Why is the driver at the front?
* Why does it have a top?
* Why doesn't it have a top?

What kind of bus do you want to make?

Talk about the kinds of buses you know about.
Have you been on a bus?
Will your teacher or another grown-up take you on a bus?

single-deckers

double-deckers

mini-buses

open-top buses

* Which takes the most passengers?
* Which takes the fewest passengers?

Paint pictures of what you want to make.
This will help you plan how to make your model.

Making the body of the bus

You will need

boxes from the junk box

What kind of box will you need for the body of the bus?

Ask yourself some questions.

* Who is the bus for?
* What kind of bus is it going to be?
* Should the box be
    strong/bendable?
    easy to cut/hard to cut?
    tall/short?
    wide/narrow?

Tell the class why you have chosen your particular box.

shoe box
a school bus?

cornflakes box
a single-decker?

small box
a mini-bus?

up-turned box with no lid
a sight-seeing bus?

Activity 7

Sticking things together

You will need to stick things together when making your model.

Perhaps you want to make a bus out of 2 boxes.
Perhaps you want to stick things onto your bus.

You will need

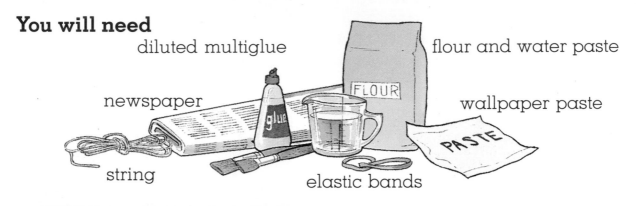

diluted multiglue

flour and water paste

newspaper

wallpaper paste

string

elastic bands

Touch the sticky substances.
* Are they too sticky? Do your fingers get stuck together? Add more water.
* Are they not sticky enough? Add more glue.

Stick objects together.

Try wrapping difficult objects together in newspaper and paste to make them stick.

Why do we have wheels?

Look at a bus carefully.

Ask some questions.
* What makes the bus move?
* What sort of wheels has it got?
* How many has it got?
* Why do buses have wheels?

Look at different kinds of wheels.
How many types can you see?
Look outside at the traffic.

Activity 9

Moving and rolling

Problem

We need to move a bus and a passenger across the classroom floor.

You will need

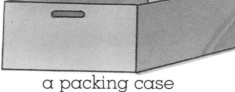

objects which can act as rollers

a packing case

A packing case can be a bus in this experiment. Someone sit in the case and pretend to be the passenger.

Think about the problem. Can you think of any solutions?
Ideas! Ideas! Ideas!
Test out your best ideas.

Think about wheels. Put rollers underneath the case.
Rounders poles or broom handles are good ideas.

What is it about a roller which solves the problem?
Think about the shape.

Let's look at wheels

Are you going to put wheels on to your bus? What can you use for wheels?

Collect objects you can use for wheels

Can you think of some more?
Test them to see if they would work as wheels.

Ideas for Wheel Tests

1) Roll each object down a plank of wood.

Watch how it moves.

Watch how far it moves.

2) Roll each one on different types of floor surfaces.

Roll on tiles.

Roll on carpet.

✳ What differences do you find?
✳ Why do you think there are differences?

Sort your objects into things we can use and things we can't use.

11

Activity 11

The wheels on the bus

You will need

objects which could be used as wheels

Choose what objects you are going to use for the wheels. Tell the class why you have chosen them.

How are you going to fix them on to your bus?

You could stick them on to the bus.
What problem do you find?

You could use axles.
Look at a toy car. How are the wheels held on?

You could make an axle like the one on the toy car.

You will need
tools
dowel

Make holes in the wheels using the tools.

Be careful

For help with these tools, see "Snow White and the seven dwarfs".

Problem solving with axles

Problem

How do you fix the axles to the bus?

Think of ideas to solve this problem.

You will need

cotton reels

plastic tubes

tools

Making a hole in the bus

Sticking tubes on to the bus

Problem

The wheels keep falling off the axle.

How can you keep the wheels on the axle?

Test out the best ideas.

You will need

elastic bands

plasticine

dowels

Activity 13

Cleaning up!

Is your model messy? Have a look.
Clean it up to make it look attractive and to make sure it works properly.

We could

wipe away glue

cover up glue or dirty marks with paper

trim the models with scissors

smooth rough parts with sand paper

Test your model for strength. Push it! Are there any weaknesses?

Strengthen the parts which are weak.

Think up ideas of how you can do this.

You could use pieces of wood, sawn to the right size and stuck down to strengthen the weak parts.

On the bus

Talk to the rest of your class about your model.

* Where will your windows go?
* Where will your doors go? How many doors will there be?
* How many passengers can fit into your bus?

Make some models of passengers.

You will need

small things

things which will
cut easily

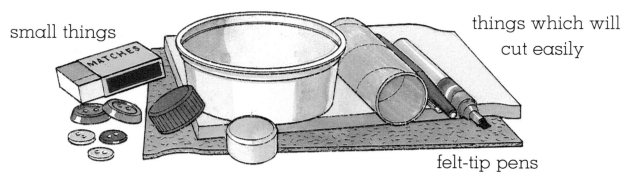

felt-tip pens

Find the right size and shape for your passenger models.
Test them in your bus.

How can you make them look like passengers?

Activity 15

Decorating your bus

Decorate your bus to make it look attractive.
You will also be helping to protect it.

You will need

varnish   paint   sticky paper   crayons

Use sticky paper for windows and doors. Cut out window shapes and door shapes.
Paint your model. It will make your model look better and will hide any messy bits.

What colour are you going to paint it? Different paints can make it a happy bus, a busy bus, a work bus, a holiday bus.

Which will yours be? Use crayons on top of the painted surface. Draw a number on the front of your bus.

Do you want to varnish your model? It will make it look glossy. It will also help to protect it from knocks and other materials spilling on to it.

Is your bus a good invention? Tell everyone why.